PUBLISH A BOOK IN 24-48 HOURS AND MAKE MONEY.

PAGE 1
INTRODUCTION

PAGE 2
COPYRIGHT

PAGE 3
WHAT IS NEEDED?

PAGE 4
FREE RESOURCES.

PAGE 5
IDEAS ON HOW TO GET PAID.

PAGE 6
HOW TO GET STARTED IN PUBLISHING A BOOK?

PAGES 7-101
AFFIRMATIONS

PAGE 102
AUTHOR BIOGRAPHY

PAGE 103-112
INSPIRATION PICTURES

Introduction:

This book will help anyone publish a book quickly, professionally and fast. And also learn simple ways to make money having a book published. Free resources available to help make the publishing less cost and more profitable. It is time to boss up ladies and gentlemen. It is possible. Thanks for your support.

Copyright © 2021 Joy Jallah

All rights reserved. In accordance with the U.S. Copyright Act of 1976, the scanning, uploading, and electronic sharing of any part of this book without the permission of the publisher is unlawful piracy and theft of the author's intellectual property. If you would like to use material from the book (other than for review purposes), prior written permissions must be obtained by contacting the publisher at joyfullypublishing@yandex.com

WEBSITE:

http//www.everra.com/store/glowing

OR
SOCIAL MEDIA INFO:
https://www.facebook.com/joyfully.jallah11

ISBN: 9798596115000

What is needed?

1. Computer or Laptop
2. Email
3. Journal or Notebook
4. Dropbox (www.dropbox.com)

Free Resources to publish a book:
Go to www.canva.com
Help with Book Cover, business logo, Facebook Post, Presentation, Instagram stories, and more.

Go to www.kdp.com
Self Publishing website.
Publish Kindle.
Publish Paperback.

Ideas on how to get paid?

Social Media: Instagram, Tiktok, Twitter, Facebook.

Ideas on how to get paid?

　　1. Cashapp
　　2. Paypal
　　3. Cash

How to get started in publishing a book?
1. Have your writing ready.
2. Go to www.dropbox.com
3. Go to www.canva.com
4. Go to www.kdp.com
5. Go to Email

Please email me, let me know you will like to get started in publishing your book and need 15 minutes free coaching. Over 15 minutes of coaching there is a fee that will be due before more coaching.

joyfullypublishingcompany@yandex.com
Free 15 minutes coaching available.

AFFIRMATIONS

I am happy & grateful now I am making money.

Affirmation: The fruit of my hands are bless.

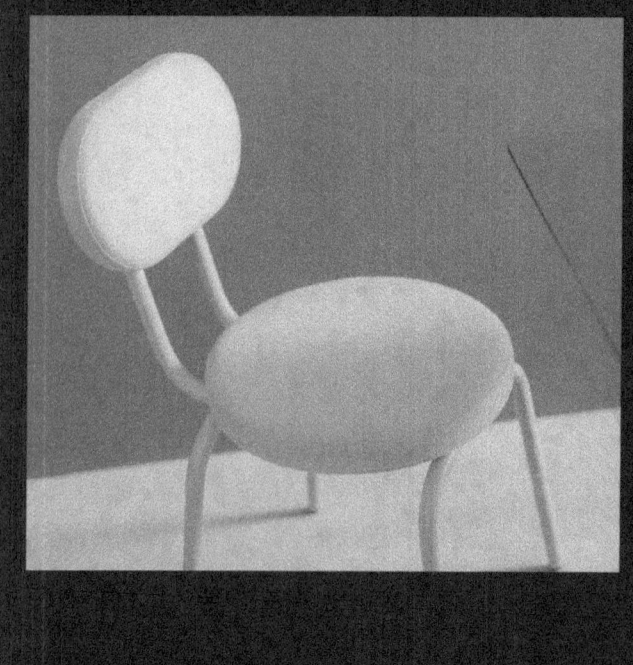

Affirmation: The fruit of my hands are bless.

Affirmation:

I am happy & grateful now. I have peace of mind in all I do.

Affirmation:

I am happy & grateful now. Business Partners & Customers are joining my team.

Affirmation:

I am happy & grateful now. I have peace of mind in all I do.

I am happy and grateful now. I am financially free.

Affirmation:

I am happy & grateful now. My relationships are healthy.

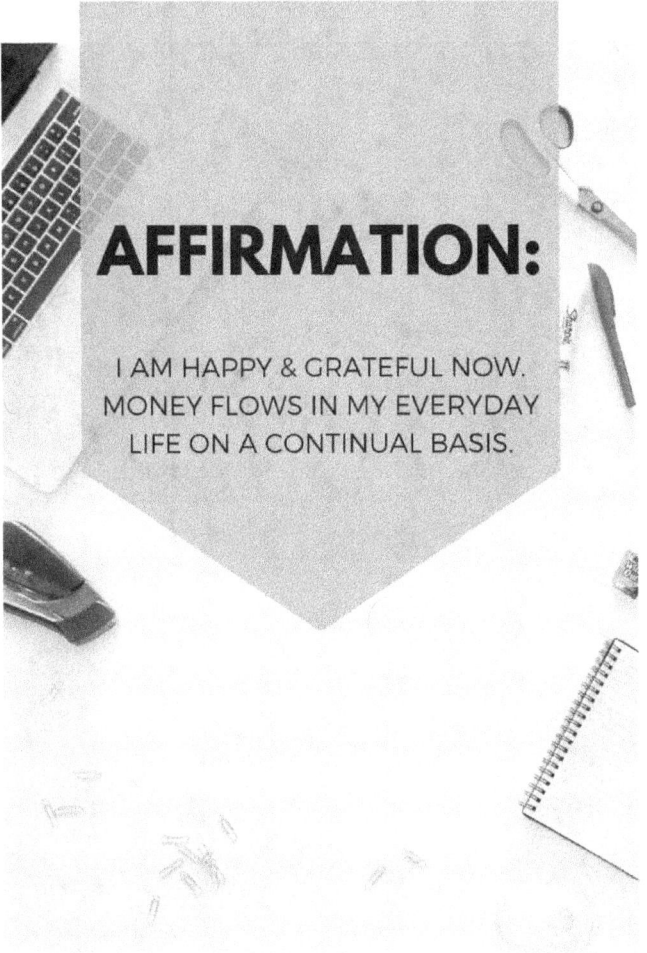

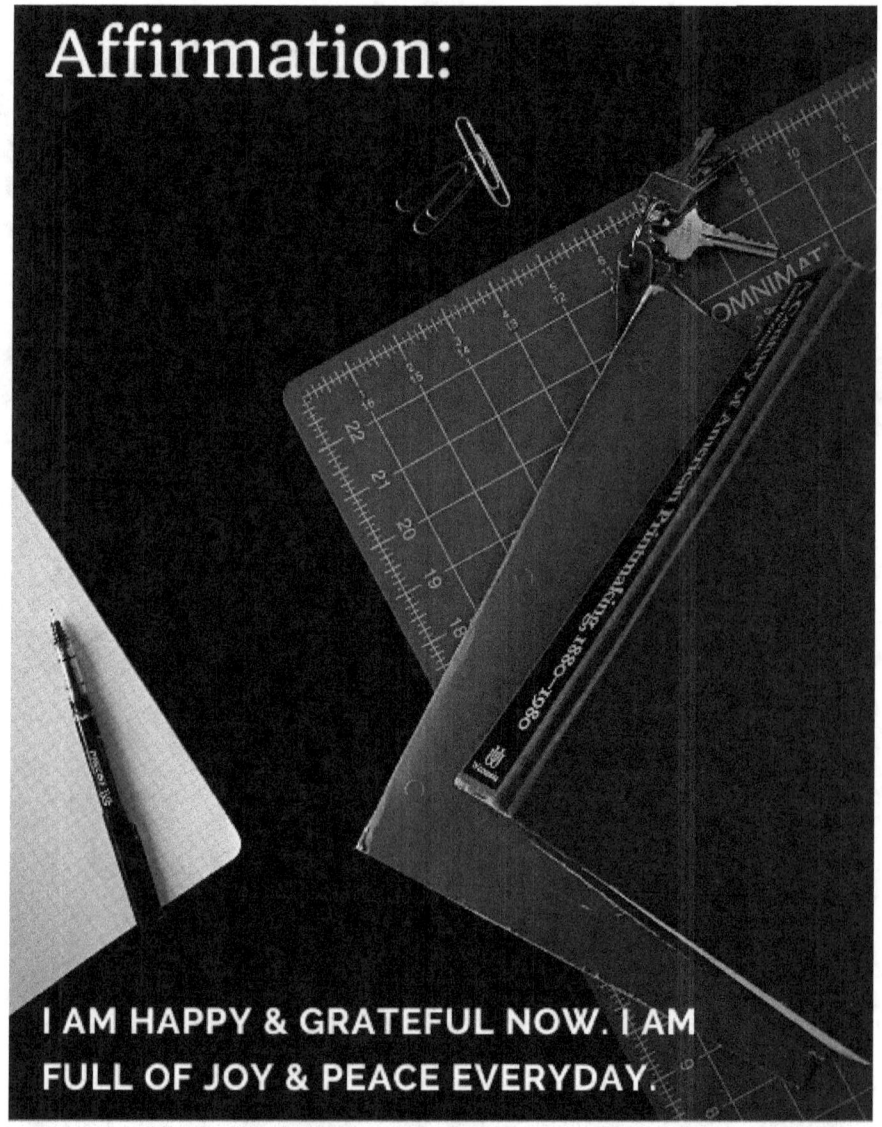

AFFIRMATION:
I AM HAPPY & GRATEFUL NOW. I HAVE SUCCESS IN MY BUSINESSES.

AFFIRMATION:

I am happy & grateful now. I am financially independence.

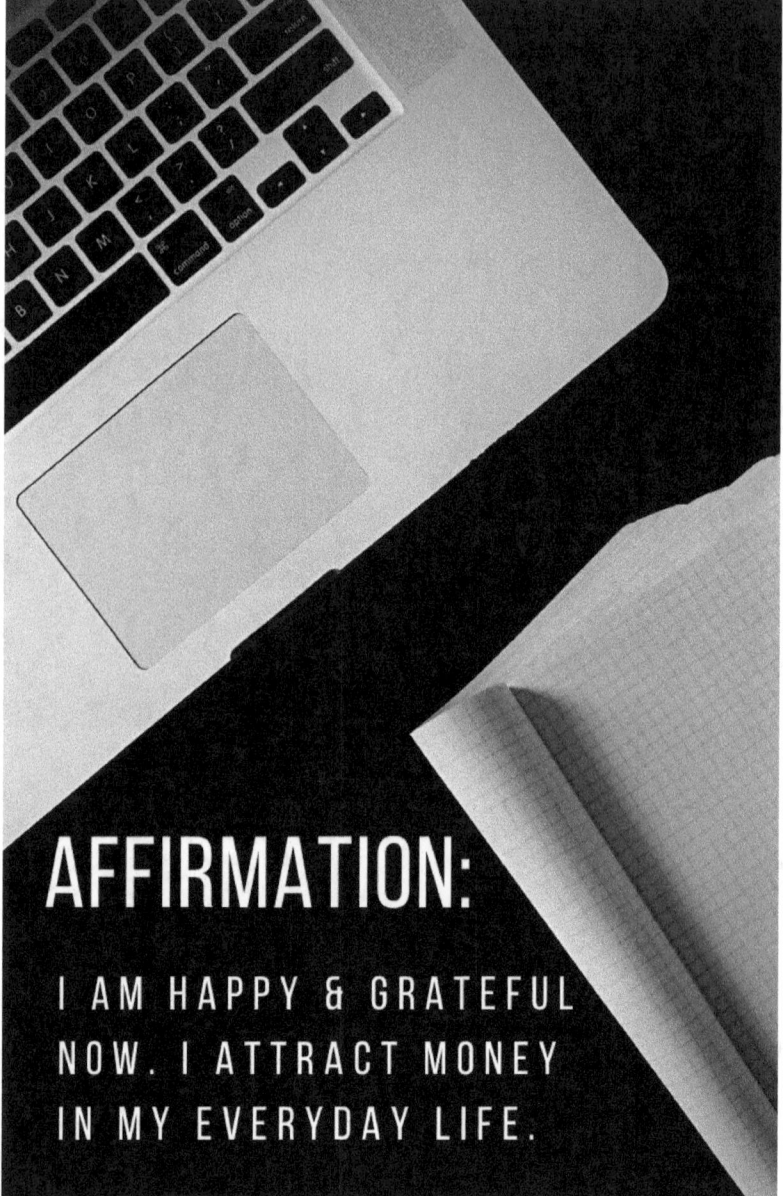

Affirmation:

I am happy & grateful now.
My relationships are healthy.

Affirmation:
I am happy and grateful now. I am peaceful everyday.

Affirmation:

I AM HAPPY &
GRATEFUL NOW. I
ATTRACT GOOD
CONNECTIONS
THAT BRING
VALUE IN MY LIFE.

AFFIRMATION:

I AM HAPPY & GRATEFUL NOW. I LIVE A LIFE OF UNLIMITED POSSIBILITIES.

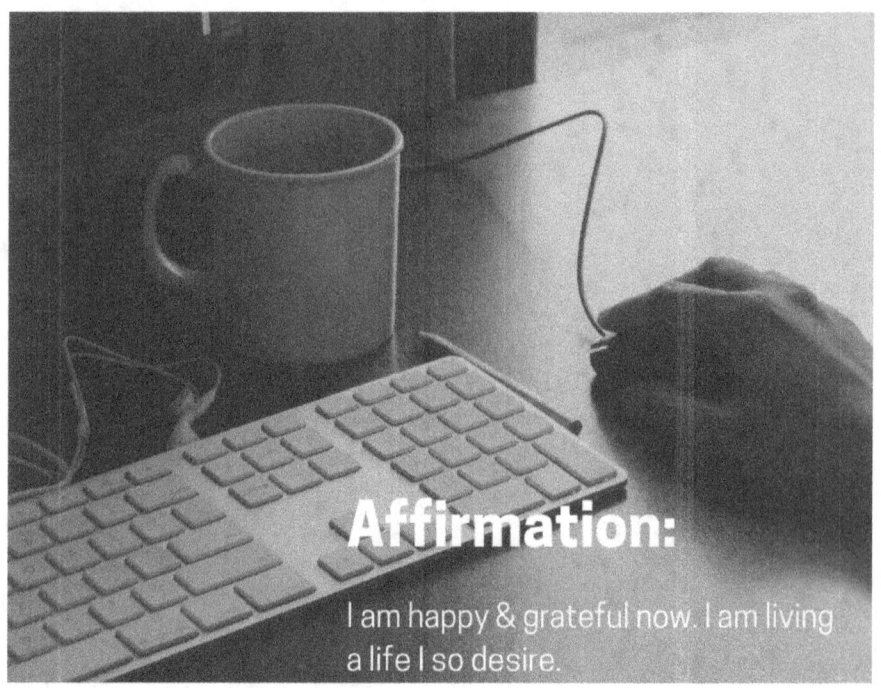

Affirmation:

I am happy & grateful now.
My life bring joy to others.

Affirmation:

I am happy & grateful now. I am living in abundance.

I am happy & grateful now. Money comes to me in multiple sources in a continual basis.

I AM HAPPY & GRATEFUL NOW. EVERYTHING I TOUCH TO DO PROSPERS.

AFFIRMATION:
I AM HAPPY & GRATEFUL NOW. MY DREAMS ARE MY REALITY.

AFFIRMATION:
I am happy & grateful now. I attraction abundance of blessings.

**Affirmation:
I am happy &
grateful now.
I am whole
and well.**

AFFIRMATION:

I am happy & grateful now. I have destiny helpers in my daily life.

Affirmation: I am happy & grateful now. I am financially free.

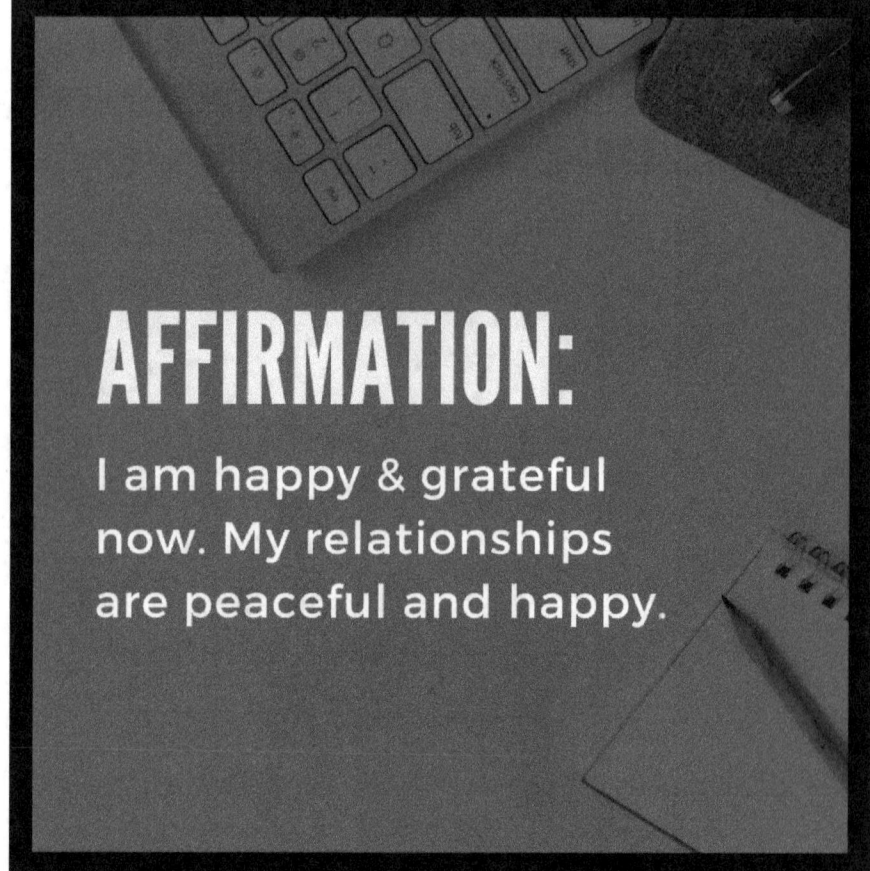

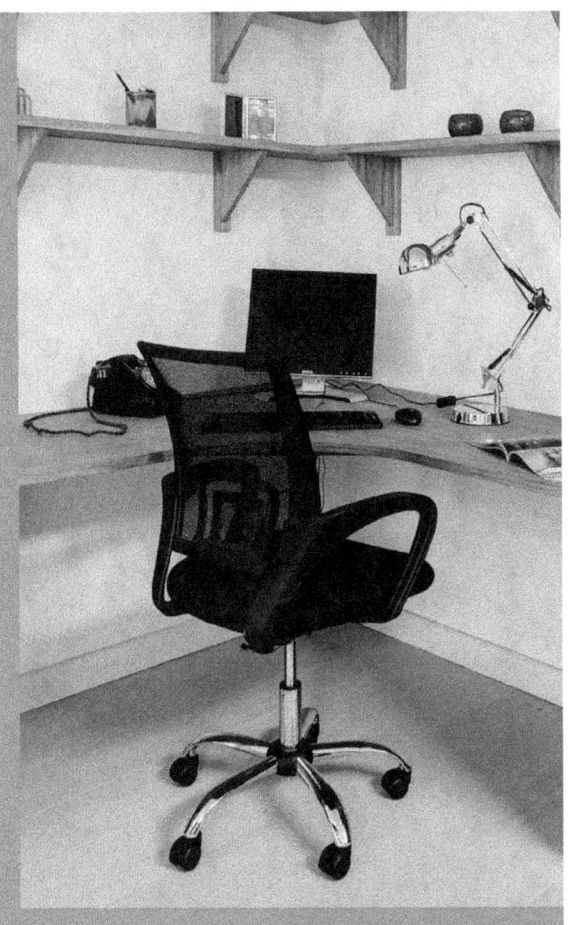

Affirmation:

I am happy & grateful now. I am so full of love for others.

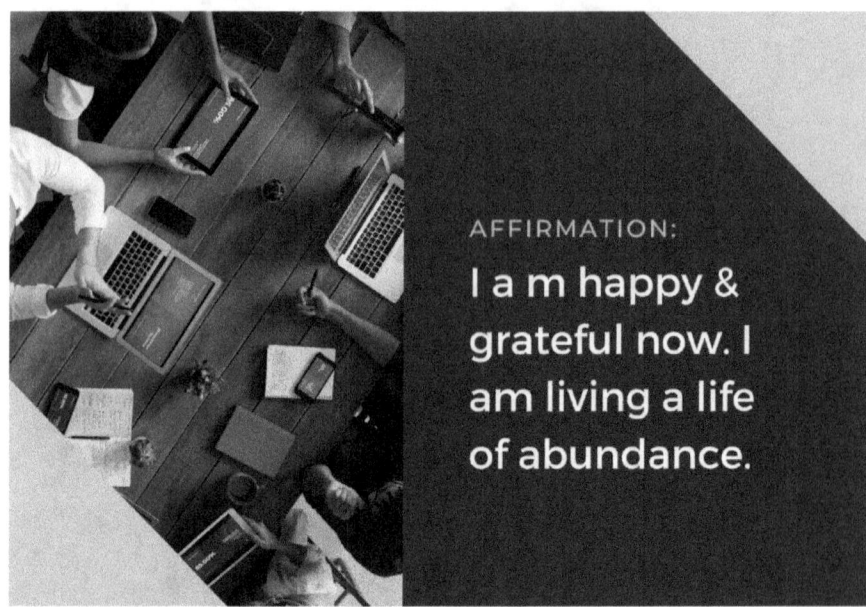

AFFIRMATION:

I a m happy & grateful now. I am living a life of abundance.

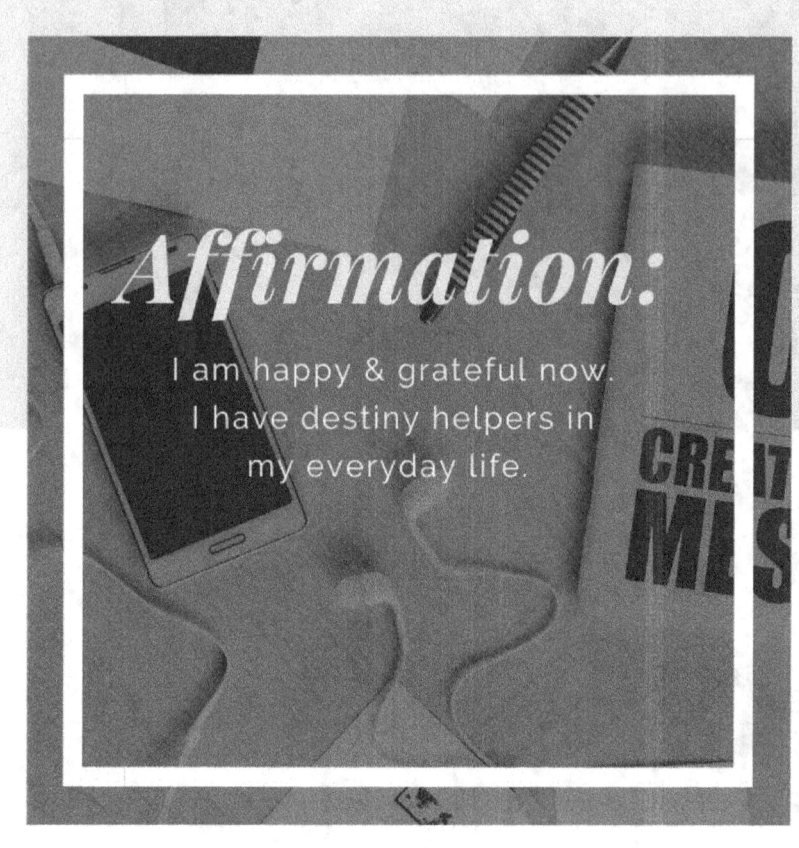

Affirmation:

I am happy & grateful now. I am grateful that a live a relax life.

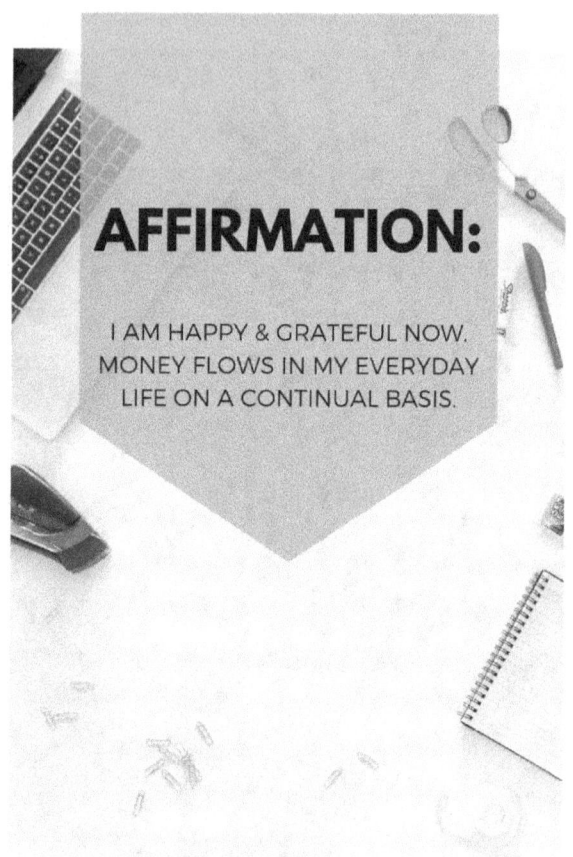

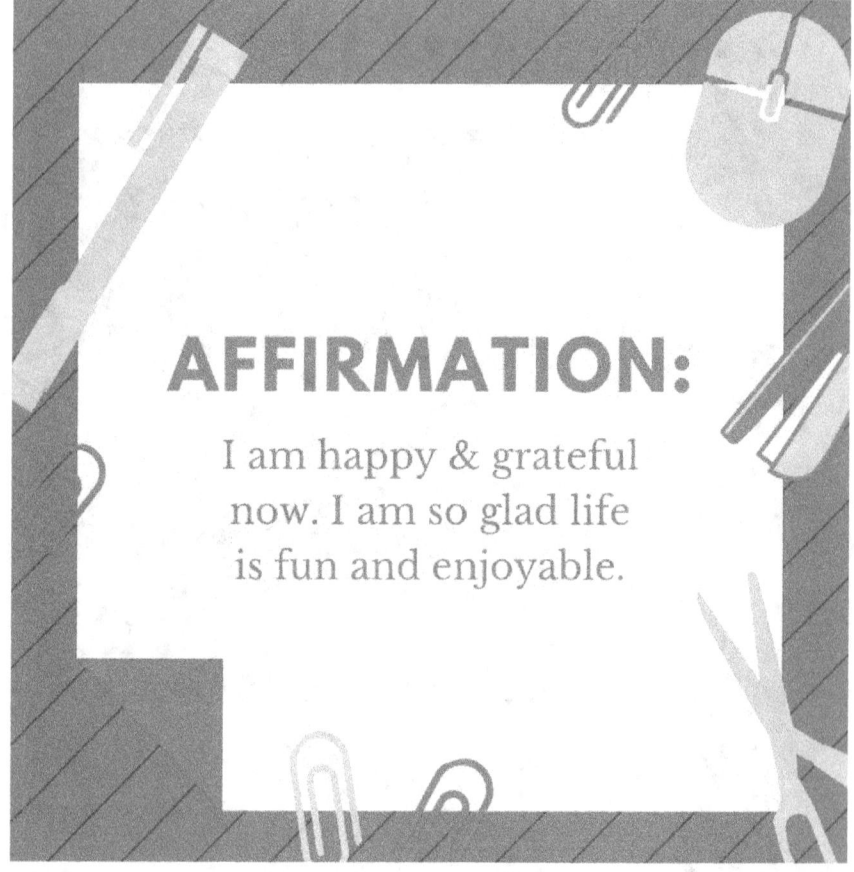

AFFIRMATION:

I am happy & grateful now. I am so glad life is fun and enjoyable.

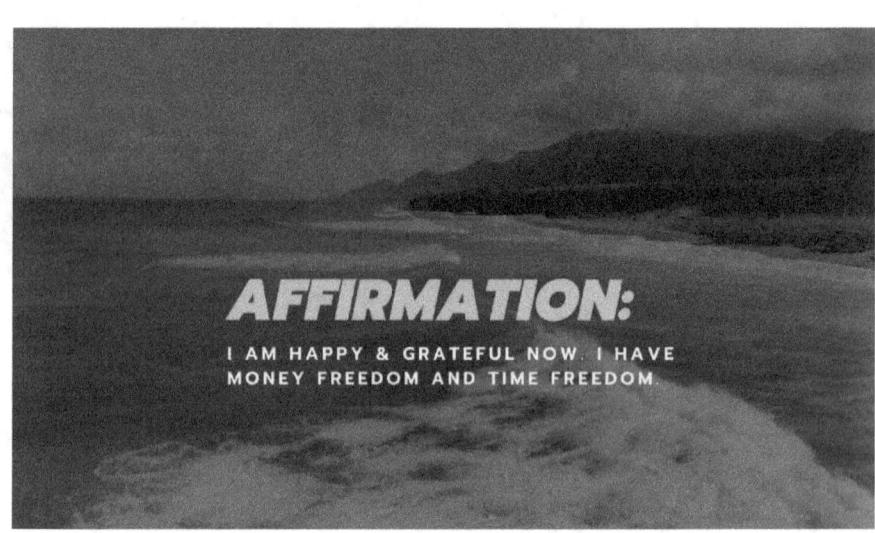

Affirmation:

I am happy & grateful now. I am peaceful in my mind, body, and spirit.

Affirmation:
I am happy & grateful now. I am living a life of excellence.

Affirmation:
I am happy
&grateful now ~~I~~
am wealthy.

Affirmation:
I am happy &
grateful now. I have
more than enough
in my everyday life.

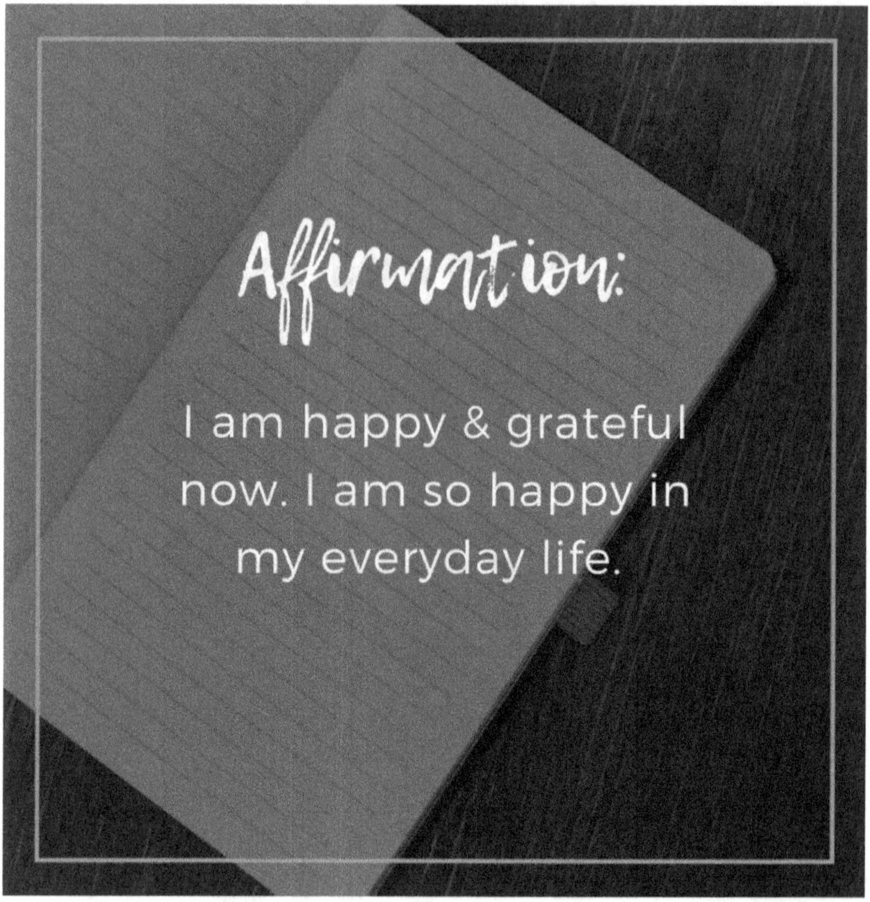

Affirmation:

I am happy & grateful now. I am so happy in my everyday life.

AFFIRMATION:

I am happy & grateful now. I am so grateful to have a peaceful family life.

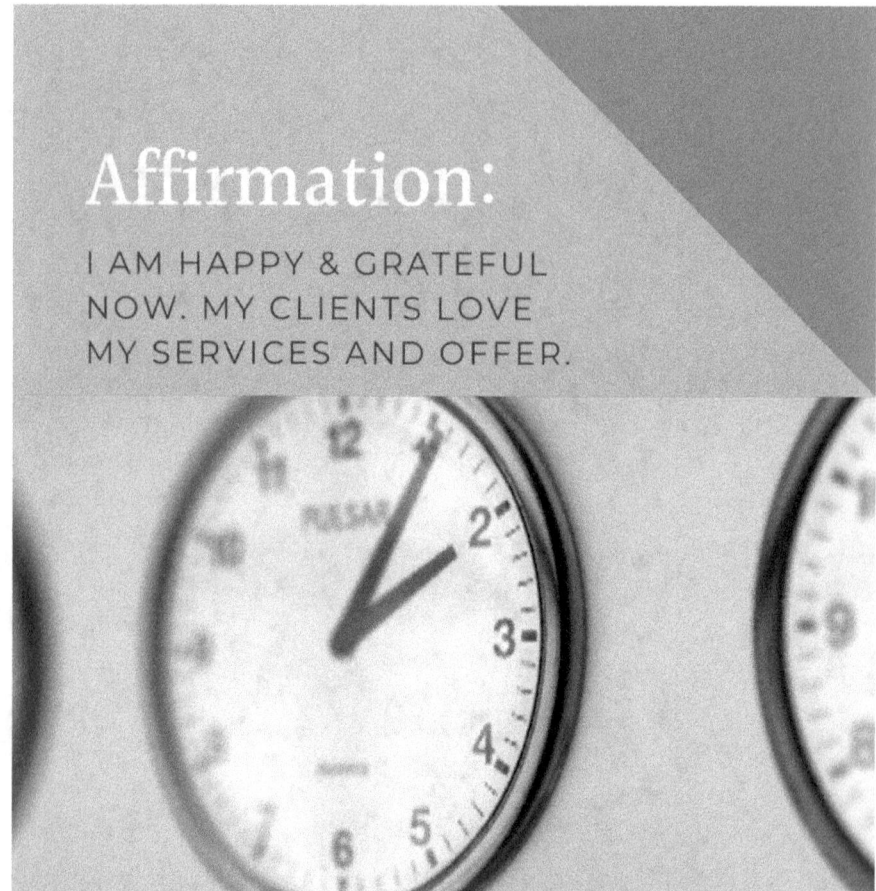

Affirmation:

I AM HAPPY & GRATEFUL NOW. MY CLIENTS LOVE MY SERVICES AND OFFER.

I am happy & grateful now. My clients are life time customers.

AFFIRMATION:
I AM HAPPY & GRATEFUL NOW. I MAKE MULTIPLE STREAMS OF INCOME ON A CONTINUAL BASIS.

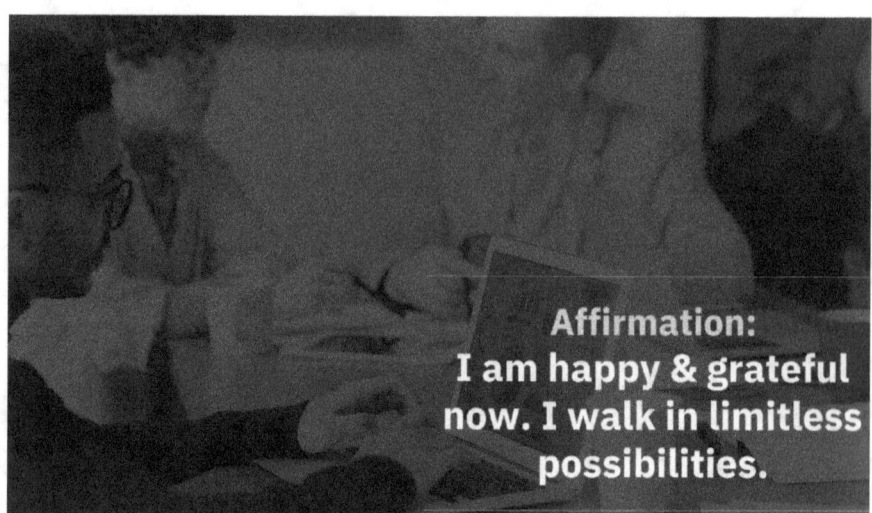

Affirmation:
I am happy & grateful now. I walk in the spirit of excellence.

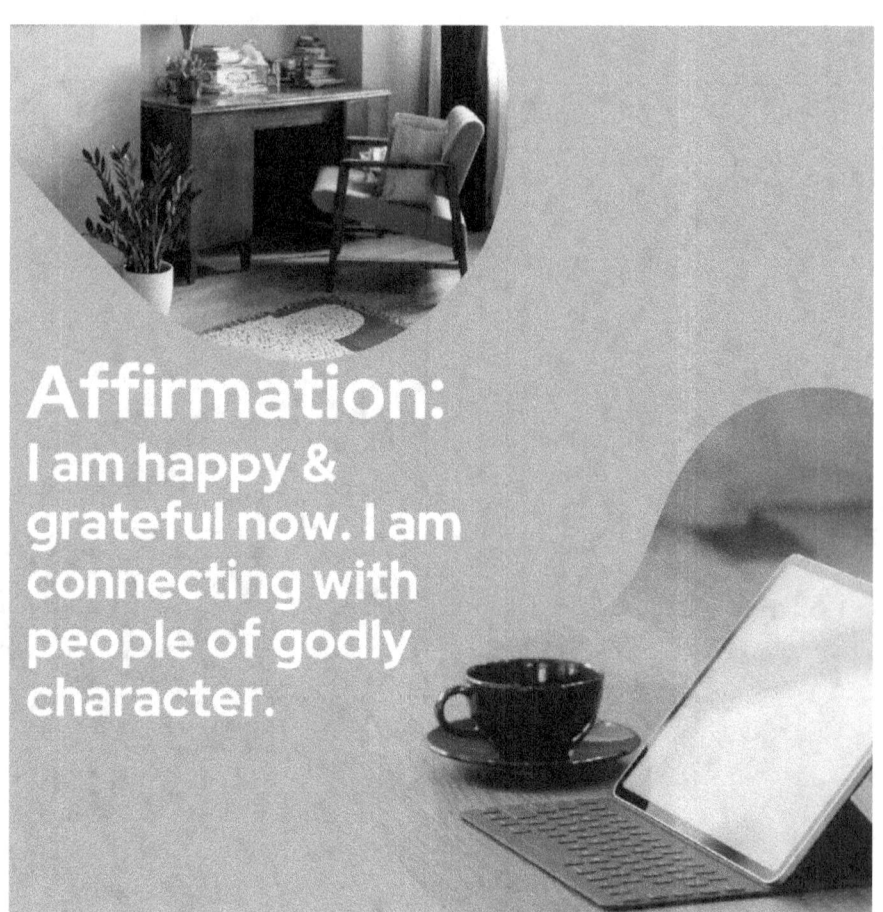

AFFIRMATION:

I AM HAPPY & GRATEFUL NOW, I AM ATTRACTING PEOPLE THAT ARE GENUINE IN MY LIFE.

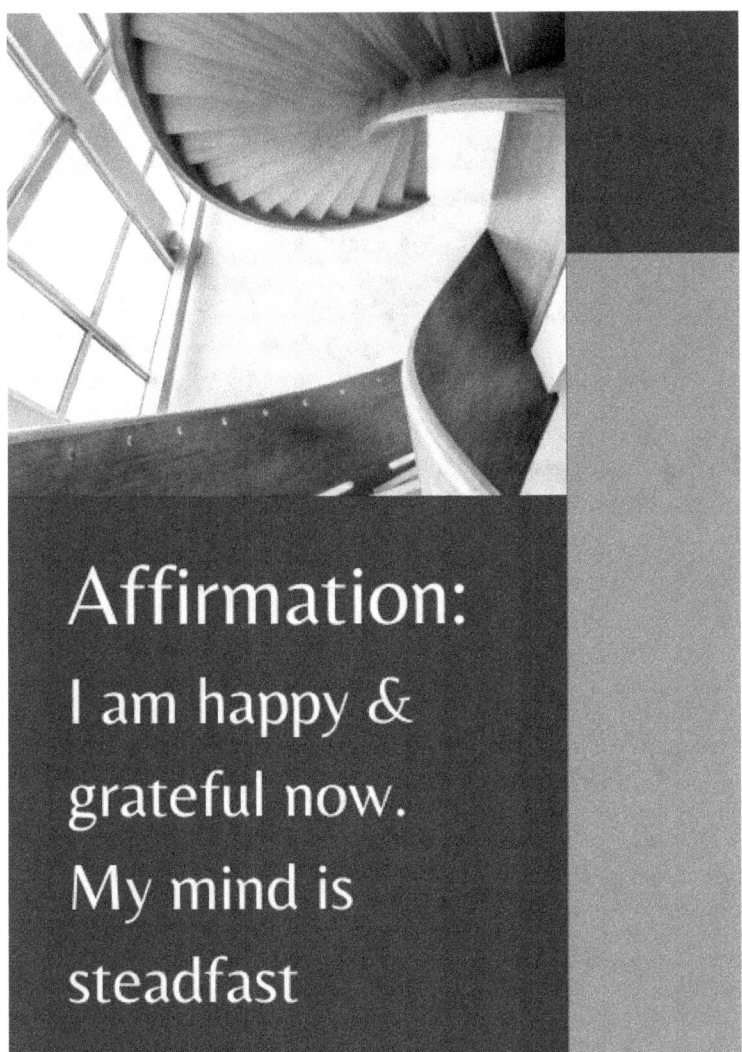

Affirmation:
I am happy & grateful now. My mind is steadfast

Affirmation:
I am happy & grateful now. I am solid in making wise decision.

Affirmation:
I am happy & grateful now. I am hopeful.

> Affirmation:
> I am happy & grateful now.
> I am so full of life.

Affirmation:
I am happy & grateful now. I so well please with living a life that please God.

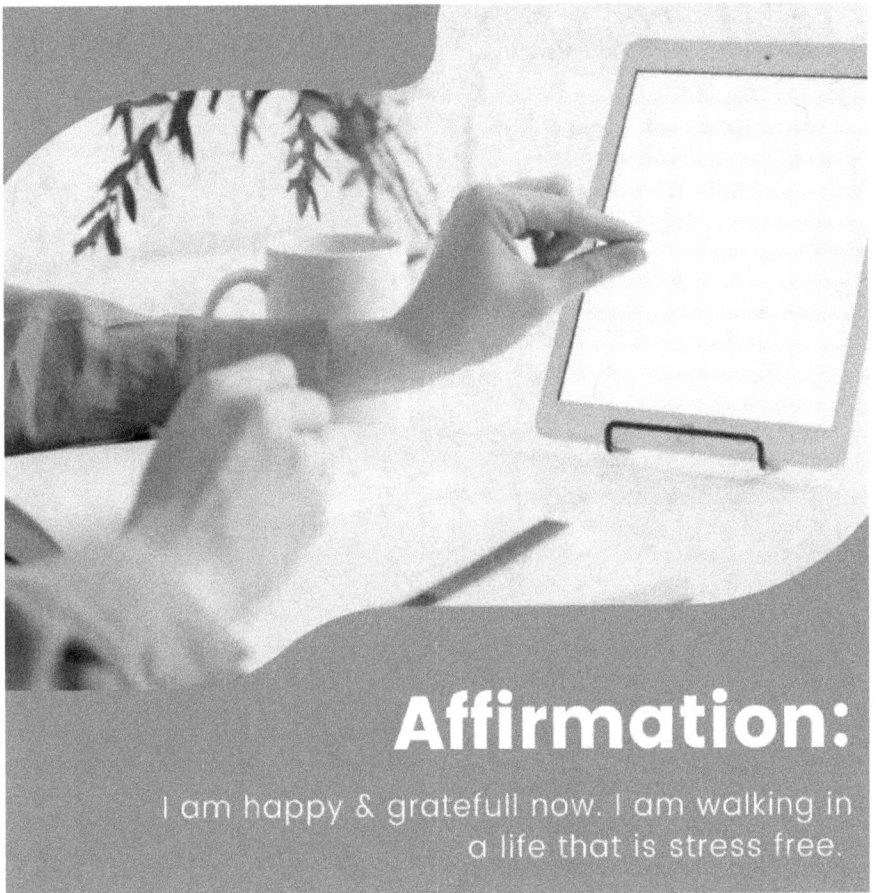

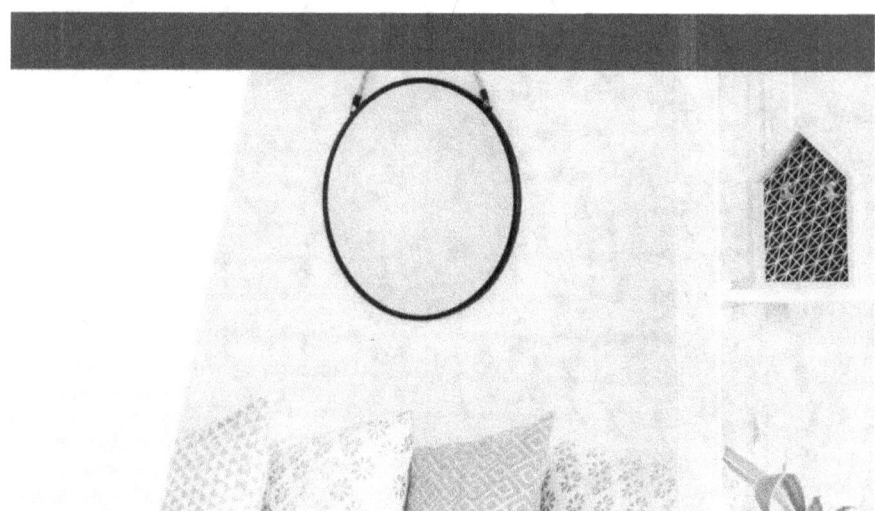

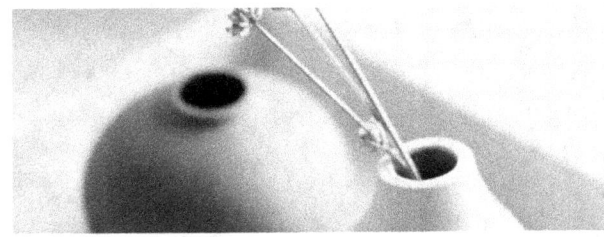

Affirmation:

I am happy & grateful now. I am completely free financially.

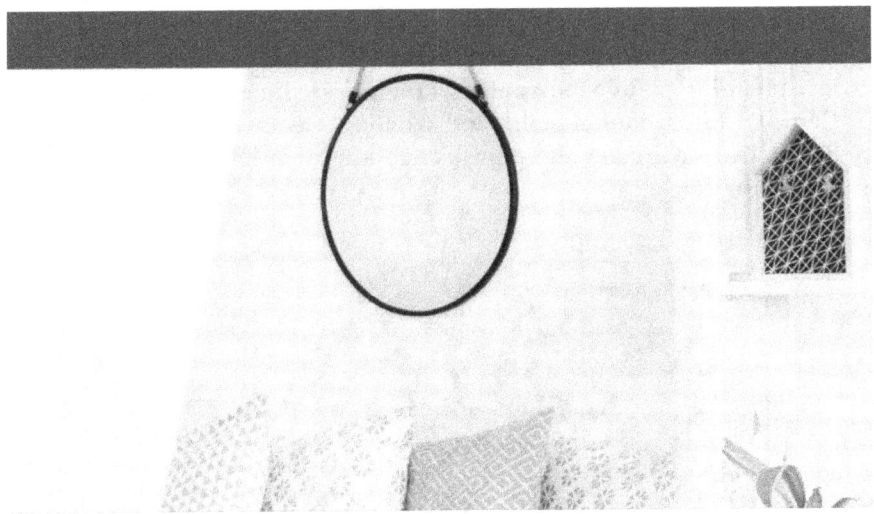

Joy Jallah

1 Bestselling Author. She loves fun and enjoys helping people get healthy. She enjoys giving back to the community. She is a mom. She loves helping people look and feel their best. She is a professional Certified Life Coach, Health and Wellness Coach. She is an Influencer. She is also a Minister and enjoys encouraging others to live a better quality of life.

Thank you for all your support. Please share your feedback.
Email:
joyfullypublishingcompany@yandex.com

Publisher :

JOYFULLY PUBLISHING

joyfullypublishingcompany@yandex.com

Enjoying Sex in Marriage

#1 BESTSELLING AUTHOR JOY JALLAH

DEEP LOVE

www.ingramcontent.com/pod-product-compliance
Lightning Source LLC
Chambersburg PA
CBHW071423210526
45465CB00001B/500